Elephants

Paul May

OXFORD
UNIVERSITY PRESS

This book belongs to:

OXFORD
UNIVERSITY PRESS

Great Clarendon Street, Oxford OX2 6DP
Oxford University Press is a department of the University of Oxford.
It furthers the University's objective of excellence in research, scholarship,
and education by publishing worldwide in

Oxford   New York

Auckland   Cape Town   Dar es Salaam   Hong Kong   Karachi
Kuala Lumpur   Madrid   Melbourne   Mexico City   Nairobi
New Delhi   Shanghai   Taipei   Toronto

With offices in

Argentina   Austria   Brazil   Chile   Czech Republic   France   Greece
Guatemala   Hungary   Italy   Japan   Poland   Portugal   Singapore
South Korea   Switzerland   Thailand   Turkey   Ukraine   Vietnam

Oxford is a registered trade mark of Oxford University Press
in the UK and in certain other countries

Text © Paul May
Illustrations © Gian Paolo Faleschini
The moral rights of the author have been asserted

Database right Oxford University Press (maker)

This edition 2009

British Library Cataloguing in Publication Data

Data available

ISBN: 978-0-19-911928-8

1 3 5 7 9 10 8 6 4 2

Printed in China
Paper used in the production of this book is a natural,
recyclable product made from wood grown in sustainable forests.
The manufacturing process conforms to the environmental
regulations of the country of origin.

Contents

▶ An elephant family

An old grandmother elephant is walking through the long grass. She is the leader of her family. Her daughters and her granddaughters walk quietly behind her.

The elephants stop. Babies hide from the sun between the legs of the grown-ups. White bones lie on the ground – elephant bones.

The elephants lift the bones with their trunks, and hold them. No one is sure why elephants do this. Perhaps they are remembering a friend.

The grandmother rumbles. Her rumbling voice is so low that only an elephant can hear it. Then the family moves off across the plain.

At the waterhole

The grandmother leads her family to the waterhole. Other elephants are there already. The elephants are excited to see each other. They put their trunks in each other's mouths to say hello. They smell each other. They squeak, they snort, they trumpet – and they drink.

Elephants love water. They suck up water in their trunks and spray each other. They swim!

Then they roll in the mud. This is fun, but it is useful too. An elephant's skin is two centimetres thick, but it burns easily in the sun. Mud is like sun cream for elephants!

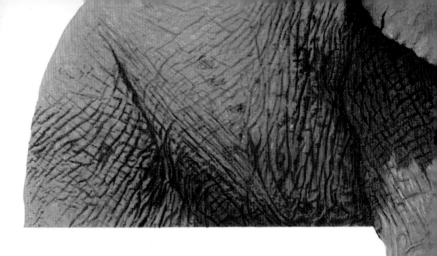

▶ Female… and male

Later, beside the waterhole, a baby
elephant is born. She is covered with
hair, and she wobbles when she tries
to stand.

The baby's mother helps her. Her
relations gather round. They sniff
the baby gently with their trunks.
They are getting to know her!

Female elephants always stay with
their mothers – even when they are
grown-up and have babies of their
own!

Male elephants don't live with the
females – they leave home when
they are about fourteen years old.
But when a female wants a mate,
males come from far and near.

Male elephants show off. They push
down trees to show how strong they
are. They trumpet and stamp.
They fight each other –

CRASH!

The winner stays with the female elephant, but he doesn't stay long. Three days pass, and then he's off again, back to his peaceful life.

Inside the female, very slowly, a new baby begins to grow. But it won't be born this year – or even next! It will be nearly two years before the baby is born.

▶ Spot the difference

Once, wild elephants lived almost everywhere in our world. Now they live in just two places, Africa and Asia.

African male

Asian male

Did you know...

A male African elephant is the biggest animal that lives on land. An adult can be 3.5 metres tall, and sometimes even taller!

An Asian male is smaller – about 3 metres tall. Female elephants are smaller than males.

Asian female

African female

Look at these elephants. They are the same age and the same size. Can you spot the difference?

Look at the elephants' backs.
They are different shapes.

Asian

African

Now check their ears. All elephants have big ears, but the ears of an African elephant are the biggest ears in the world.

African

Asian

Look closely at the elephants' trunks. One 'finger' or two?

African

Asian

Now inspect their feet – an Asian elephant often has more toenails. But don't be fooled by those big flat feet. They are like enormous shoes.

Asian

African

Look at the elephant's bones and you will see a surprising thing. Elephants walk on tiptoe!

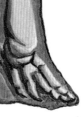

Ears

Big ears are great for listening. An elephant could hear *you* coming a kilometre away. It can hear another elephant from 4 kilometres or more!

Elephants don't just use their ears for listening: they use them to keep themselves cool, they use them as sunshades, and they use them to make themselves look even bigger than they really are. They would rather scare you than fight with you!

▶ Trunks...

Inside an elephant's trunk there are tens of thousands of muscles. A trunk can sniff the wind for the smell of danger – or the smell of a friend. It could smell *you* coming from a kilometre away!

A trunk can:

touch!

squirt!

snorkel...

...pick up
tree trunks...

or tiny
seeds...

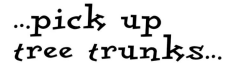

and
trumpet!

But most important of all,
an elephant uses its trunk
to eat and drink.

...and teeth!

Elephants only sleep for about four hours each night. The rest of the time – all day and most of the night – they eat! Elephants aren't fussy eaters. They like fruit best, but they will eat leaves, grass, roots, and even bark.

Inside an elephant's mouth there are only four teeth. Each tooth is as big as a brick and as rough as a cheese grater.

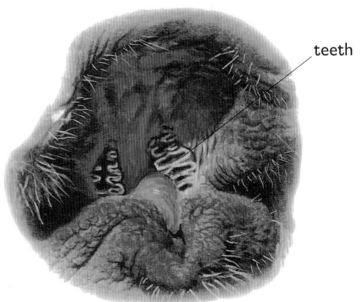

teeth

Every day an elephant grinds up more than 150 kilos of food. Those enormous teeth wear out – but that's fine. Another set is waiting to replace them. An elephant wears out six sets of teeth before it dies!

▶ Tusks

Most elephants have two long front teeth as well. Only female Asian elephants do not have tusks. Tusks are an elephant's tools. A tusk can be a spade, or a knife, or even a trunk-rest!

Tusks can be terrible weapons, too.
Elephants don't fight often – but
when they do, they are terrifying.

a baby elephant rests
against her mother

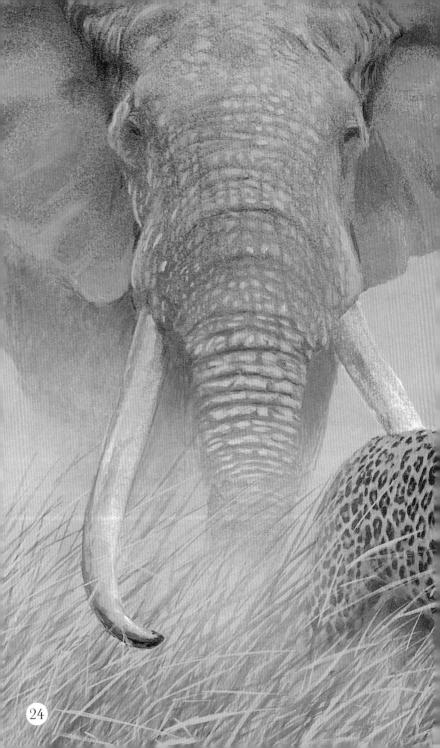

A baby African elephant has strayed from his family. A leopard crouches in the long grass. The leopard would not dare to attack the baby's mother. But it will kill the baby if it can.

The leopard creeps closer. Suddenly the mother elephant turns and sees it. She charges. She stamps with one enormous foot, and she slashes at the leopard with her tusks. The leopard flees – and the baby is safe.

▶ Remembering

This elephant has fallen to the ground. She has lived for 60 years but now her last set of teeth has worn out. She cannot eat properly, and she is very tired.

Her daughters and her granddaughters gather round. They stroke her with their trunks. They try to pull her to her feet, but she is too weak to stand.

They leave her to die in peace.

Many years pass. The wind blows and the hot sun beats down. The elephant's bones lie in the long grass, but her family do not forget her.

Whenever they pass by, they stop. Babies hide from the sun between the legs of the grown-ups. The elephants lift the bones in their trunks. They hold them – and they remember.

▶ Glossary

 rumble A rumble is a noise that elephants make, which is so low that only other elephants can hear it.   **5**

 waterhole A waterhole is a pool of water where animals drink and wash themselves. **6, 8**

 mate A mate is one of a pair of animals that have come together to have babies.   **9**

 tusk A tusk is a long, pointed tooth that sticks out of the mouth of an elephant.
22, 23, 25

 trunk A trunk is an elephant's long, flexible nose.
4, 6, 7, 8, 15, 18, 19, 22, 27, 29

trumpet A loud noise that an elephant makes. **6, 10, 19**

 snorkel To snorkel is to use a tube to breathe whilst under water. **19**

OXFORD

WILD READS

WILD READS will help your child develop a love of reading and a lasting curiosity about our world. See the websites and places to visit below to learn more about elephants.

Elephants

WEBSITES

http://www.bbc.co.uk/cbbc/wild/amazinganimals/

http://www.wwf.org.uk/gowild/

http://www.wwf.org.uk/core/

Adopt an elephant!
http://www.adoptwildlife.org/adopt_elephant.htm

PLACES TO VISIT

Whipsnade Zoo
http://www.zsl.org/zsl-whipsnade-zoo/

Chester Zoo
http://www.chesterzoo.org/

West Midlands Safari and Leisure Park
http://www.wmsp.co.uk/index.php

You can also see elephants in many different parts of the world such as Africa, Thailand and India.